How to Do a Belly Flop!

And Other Tricks, Tips and Skills No Adult Will Teach You

Marc Tyler Nobleman
Dave and Joe Borgenicht

Drawings by Matt Phillips

CHRYSALIS CHILDREN'S BOOKS

First published in Great Britain in 2005 by
Chrysalis Children's Books
an imprint of Chrysalis Books Group plc
The Chrysalis Building, Bramley Road
London W10 6SP
www.chrysalisbooks.co.uk

Text copyright © 2005 Quirk Packaging, Inc.
Illustrations copyright © 2005 Matt Phillips

A QUIRK PACKAGING BOOK
Editor: Sharyn Rosart, Linda A. Doeser (UK edition)
Design director: Lynne Yeamans

The moral right of the author and illustrator
has been asserted

BRITISH LIBRARY CATALOGUING-IN-PUBLICATION DATA
A catalogue record for this book is available
from the British Library.

ISBN 1 84458 416 X
Printed in China

When doing belly flops, climbing trees and other tasks in this book it is important to keep safety in
mind and parental guidance and common sense should be followed at all times.

The tips and skills in this book are based on reasonable research and are not intended to cause
injury. The Publisher and authors disclaim all liability that may result from use or reliance on the
information provided in this book. We urge you to obey all laws and respect the rights of others.

CONTENTS

PRACTICAL SKILLZ

#1 Make a Great Pizza 5
#2 Attract the Attention of the Ice Cream Van 10
#3 Make Frozen Treats 13
#4 Tell a Ghost Story 16
#5 Build a Fort 19
#6 Host a Garden Fête 24
#7 Write/Direct/Perform a Play 29
#8 Make Your Own Blockbuster 32

TRICK SKILLZ

#9 Have a Snowball Fight in July 37
#10 Perform an Amazing Card Trick 40
#11 Make a Coin Disappear 44
#12 Stand on Your Head/Do a Handstand 47

GAME SKILLZ

#13 Play Capture the Flag 51
#14 Play Hopscotch 56
#15 Play Skully 58
#16 Be an Expert at Jacks 61

WATER SKILLZ

#17 Be a Master Stone Skimmer 65
#18 Perform a Swan Dive/Jackknife/Back Dive 68
#19 Do a Cannonball 72
#20 Do a Belly Flop 74

NATURE SKILLZ

#21 Climb a Tree 77
#22 Do a Bird Call 80
#23 Camp Out in Your Garden 83
#24 Hatch a Butterfly 87
#25 Catch a Shooting Star 92

PRACTICAL

SKiLLZ

KIDSKILL #1
MAKE A GREAT PIZZA

EVERYONE LOVES PIZZA, SO THEY'LL ALL LOVE YOU. Check with a parent that it's okay to make pizzas and do clear up the kitchen afterwards if you want to be allowed to do it again. Make sure you understand how the oven works or get a parent to help with that bit.

THE GOAL:
To make a pizza with your favourite – or your friends' favourite – toppings.

Wash your hands before you start – you don't want to give everyone food poisoning. If you have long hair, tie it back and, however silly you think it makes you look, wear an apron. It's better than splashing tomato all over your favourite jeans.

THE EQUIPMENT:
For each pizza
- 25 cm ready-made pizza base
- 175 ml passata or canned tomato purée

Choose toppings from
- sliced pepperoni
- drained canned tuna
- chopped ham
- drained canned pineapple
- drained canned sweetcorn
- sliced tomato
- chopped cooked chicken
- peeled cooked prawns
- chopped spring onions
- sliced frankfurters
- grated Cheddar or sliced mozzarella cheese

THE SKILL:

1 Decide what toppings you want to put on your pizza before you start. You don't have to have cheese, but most traditional pizzas do. Don't be too ambitious – choose two or three things that go well together.

2 If you have permission, switch on the oven to 200°C or Gas Mark 6 to heat up (or ask a parent to do it for you). Check what oven setting is suggested on the pizza base packet because it may be different. If so, use that one.

3 Collect all your ingredients together. Carefully chop and/or slice anything that needs it and grate some cheese.

4 Take the pizza base out of its packet and put it on a baking sheet. Spread the top with passata or tomato purée, leaving a little gap all round the edge.

Some terrific combinations are pineapple and ham (Hawaiian), tuna and sweetcorn, chicken, tomato and sweetcorn, tuna and prawns, pepperoni and tomato and frankfurters and spring onions.

Other toppings include black olives, baked beans, sliced mushrooms, sliced onion, sliced hard-boiled egg (a bit smelly), drained canned anchovies (very salty), chopped bacon or pickled chillies (hot!!).

MR. PIZZA!

Small bases make great faces. Spread the tomato, then make eyes with pepperoni slices topped with a pea, a nose from an upside-down slice of mushroom, a mouth from an orange pepper slice, ears from half courgette slices, cheeks from slices of mozzarella and eyebrows from celery slices. Sprinkle with olive oil and cook. When you serve the pizza faces, add grated Cheddar cheese at the top of the plate for hair.

7

5 Using your clean fingers, sprinkle your chosen toppings all over the tomato, spreading them out nice and evenly. Don't pile the toppings up too much or they'll all fall off when you come to eat the pizza. Then sprinkle the cheese evenly over the top. Try not to throw it all over the baking sheet itself as it will burn on in a nasty sticky mess that someone – you – will have to wash off later.

HAIR RESTRAINT

CLEAN HANDS (UNDER GLOVES)

OVEN GLOVE

Kiss the Cook

APRON

CLEAN SOCKS (OPTIONAL)

6 At this point, the pizza needs to go in the oven, so it may be the time to call for some parental help. If you are allowed to do it yourself, open the oven door, then put on some oven gloves to protect your hands. Carefully lift the baking sheet, keeping it level and slide it into the oven. Shut the door. If you have an oven timer, set it for 20 minutes. Otherwise check the clock or your watch and note what time the pizza went into the oven and what time it will be ready.

7 When the 20 minutes are up, check that the pizza looks cooked – WITHOUT TOUCHING IT – the cheese should be golden and bubbly.

8 Either get the parent again or get ready to lift the pizza out of the oven yourself. Turn off the oven and open the door. Put on oven gloves to protect your hands – THE BAKING SHEET WILL BE VERY HOT. Grasp the sides firmly and gently lift it out of the oven and put it on the kitchen work surface. Don't put it down on a wooden table as it will leave a mark.

9 Have a big plate ready. Slide a fish slice or big flat spatula underneath the pizza and carefully lift it on to the plate. Cut the pizza into wedges with a pizza wheel, if you have one, or with a serrated knife like a bread knife.

10 Serve the wedges to your friends, but make sure that there is a slice left for you. Carry the plate carefully as freshly baked pizza has a tendency to slide off the edge if you tip it or run.

Enjoy!

Four in one: Imagine the pizza base is a clock and put one topping between 12 o'clock and 3, another between 3 and 6 o'clock, a third between 6 and 9 o'clock and a fourth between 9 and 12 o'clock.

If mum or dad has been obediently trotting in and out of the kitchen to act as your assistant chef, it would be nice if you offered them a slice of your creation to say thank you. Don't worry, they probably won't take it because they know you've made it for your friends.

KIDSKILL #2

ATTRACT THE ATTENTION OF THE ICE CREAM VAN

IS THERE A SWEETER SOUND than the jingle of the ice cream van? What a tragedy when you sprint from the house only to see the van disappearing around the corner. Here's how to ensure you'll never miss the van again.

THE GOAL:
To prepare for the coming of the ice cream van, to be sure you catch it every time.

THE EQUIPMENT:
- money
- running shoes
- bright clothes
- empty stomach (optional)

Chasing the ice cream van is healthy (after all, running is good exercise), but wolfing down ice cream every day is not. Make sure you run more often than you eat!

THE SKILL:

1 Watch and note what time the ice cream van typically putters down your street. If you can't keep watch, ask your competitors – uh, neighbours.

2 Prepare your money. Have coins or a note on a table next to the door so it's easy to grab in a banana-split second.

3 Half an hour before the van usually arrives, make sure you're dressed in bright clothing and wearing your running shoes. Be ready ahead of time in case the van is early.

If you're a cautious type, you might want to wait outside on your front step or the front lawn, cash in your pocket. Bring a book to pass the time until the van comes. This is not a good idea if you live in a busy city.

4 With the first note of that familiar ice cream van melody, be ready outside your house – even if you can't yet see the van.

5 Never bolt into the road. Always stay on the pavement or grass. When the van comes into view, wave your arms in an 'I'm hungry' rather than an 'I'm crazy' sort of way.

6 As the van approaches, turn and make eye contact with the driver. If your timing is right, he should bring the van to a stop.

If you're not confident that your bright clothing will attract the driver's attention, bring a small mirror. Use it to create a flashing glare from the summer sun. You can later use it to check your face for unsightly splotches of dried ice cream.

ice cream FREAK!

Stop ice cream man!

THE YoE The ice CREAM

7 If other kids are present, get your money ready and be prepared to strut your way to the front of the line. (This does not mean you should literally push other kids out of the way. But if you were the one who got the driver to stop, you earned the right to be first.)

8 After buying your ice cream, thank the driver for stopping. Ask if he comes at the same time every day. If you have any special requests for types of ice cream that he doesn't currently offer, make them.

What if you miss the VAN?

You have several options:

- Run like there's only one ice cream cone left on Earth, and the first one to it gets it. You just might catch up if the necessary adrenaline kicks in when you need it most.
- Cut across a garden or park to head off the van on the next street. It helps to hum music from your favourite action film as you do this.
- Go to the next neighbourhood by bike or by bumming a lift from a parent.
- If the van has a phone number on it, phone the driver and ask him to come back.
- Put a sign on your front lawn for the future: 'Attention Ice Cream Van: I am interested. Please stop!'

KIDSKILL #3
MAKE FROZEN TREATS

IF, IN THE WORST-CASE SCENARIO, you follow all the steps in
the previous entry but still miss the ice cream van, don't freak
out – it doesn't mean you have to be deprived of frozen
treats. Just make them yourself. A kid who can make yummy
frozen treats is a very popular kid.

THE GOAL:
To prepare delicious (and even
– gasp! Don't tell anyone –
healthy) frozen treats to keep
in the cold, convenient comfort
of your own freezer.

*To many frozen treat
fanatics, home-made
frozen treats are more
appealing than prepackaged
ones, since you're in
charge of what goes
into them. No mystery
ingredients: if you
want to eat frozen
polymultihydrogenate-
gooeyyeastertract, put it
in; if you don't, don't!*

THE EQUIPMENT:
- freezer
- plastic cups (style is up
  to you, but the 75 ml size
  is good)
- wooden sticks (similar to the kind used for lollipops),
  plastic spoons or cocktail sticks
- your chosen ingredients: juice (100 per cent juice, no sugar
  added, all-natural is best), yogurt, apple sauce, and/or jelly.

*This activity may be summer-centric, but it
works just as well in winter. Some people demand
frozen treats even when it's freezing outside.*

THE SKILL:

1 Gather your ingredients together. Fizzy drinks such as cola or lemonade are not part of the RDA (Recommended Deep-freeze Assortment).

2 Arrange the cups on the work surface.

3 Pour, ooze or glop your ingredients into the cups. You can make single-flavour treats or combine flavours. If you opt for the second idea, see if you can concoct a mixture whose colour was previously unknown to humankind.

For smaller treats, follow these steps using an ice cube tray instead of plastic cups. If you want your bite-sized treats to have a handle, use wooden cocktail sticks. Cover the ice cube tray with cling-film first, then stick in the cocktail sticks.

PLASTIC WRAP TOOTH PICKS →

RIGHT KIND OF STICK

WRONG KIND OF STICK

Some sweets and other ingredients won't freeze well. It's not possible to list everything that will and won't work, so experiment. Don't try the same new ingredient in every cup — if it doesn't work, you've ruined the whole batch.

4 If desired, add a dollop of something else to your cups:

Mix in some jam.

Stir in some sprinkles.

Squirt in some chocolate, vanilla, or caramel syrup.

Drop berries, chopped nuts, mini marshmallows, crushed biscuits, chocolate chips, and/or sweets into the liquid for a crunchy and scrumptious surprise.

5 Clear some space in the freezer. A good place to start: chuck anything with a use-by date before the year you were born. Place the cups in the freezer. To move them easily, first place them all on a tray or baking sheet.

Check back after at least an hour. When the liquid has begun to solidify but is not yet hard, poke a wooden stick or plastic spoon into the centre of each cup's contents. Make sure the sticks or spoons stand upright.

6 When you're ready for a treat, remove a cup from the freezer. Push on the bottom of the cup to release the treat. The treats can be slippery, so hold on to the handle and have your mouth open and ready to catch any falling frozen pieces.

Don't pull on the wooden stick or plastic spoon handle to get the treat out of the cup, in case it is loose. Also, don't eat the handle, but licking it is okay.

KIDSKILL #4
TELL A GHOST STORY

NO CAMPFIRE or Halloween sleepover is complete without
a chilling tale, but you can spin a spooky story anywhere,
anytime – well, anytime of night. Telling a ghost story in day-
light is like swimming in air – it just doesn't make sense.

> You may recycle a ghost story someone else told
> you, but it's always scarier if you give your
> audience something completely new. If you're
> not good at making up entire stories, take a
> story you already know and change it around
> a bit. Instead of a dog-headed ghost with an
> appetite for pickles, make it a pickle-headed
> ghost with an appetite for dogs.

THE GOAL:
To tell a ghost story that will send a chill up (and back down)
the spines of your audience.

THE EQUIPMENT:
- your imagination
- nerves of steel
- audience
- dark room
  or spot outside
- torch(es) (optional)

Ghost stories work well when
told in a slow, hushed voice.
This makes any sudden noises
(whether from you or from
the darkness beyond you)
all the more frightening.
Don't feel strange if that's
not how you normally talk—
people expect a performance
when they agree to hear a
ghost story.

16

THE SKILL:

1 If you plan to use or modify an existing story, poke around in books or surf online to find one you like.

2 Rehearse your story privately in advance. A polished delivery is a strong delivery.

3 Decide when you will spring it on your friends. Sleepovers are great opportunities.

4 Wait as late as possible before beginning your tale. Humans tend to be more afraid as the night advances, since we seem to believe that the creepiest creatures don't come out until most people are asleep. And that doesn't mean a couple of insomniac squirrels.

5 Unleash your story in a place that is as dark as possible.

If inside, turn off all lights. If outside, lead the group to a dark spot with torches, then have everyone but you turn them off. Don't bother putting the torch under your chin and aiming the beam up at your face. That's been done so many times it's about as scary as a kitten.

= SCARY

= NOT SCARY.

6 Ask everyone to gather around you.

Every so often, stop talking for a second and look up as if you see or hear something in the distance. Don't do this in an exaggerated fashion. It's just a subtle trick to heighten people's anxiety by subconsciously suggesting that something is out there watching you. And you just know that something isn't just a sleepless rabbit.

7 At the start, imply that your story is true. This freaks people out more. Do this by giving real-life details such as 'Back in 1997 . . . ' or 'There used to be an abandoned barn where Superdrug is now. . . ' You can even connect your story to a real person or family everyone knows by saying something like 'My neighbour Elizabeth heard this story from her cousin.'

8 Up the scare factor by saying something like 'Supposedly everyone who hears this story will be cursed, but I don't believe that.' No matter how scared people get, don't stop, and don't say, 'It's just a story.' If they agreed to listen, they have to stick it out to the end.

9 End the story with a freaky, present-day phenomenon such as 'People today still hear moaning sounds when they go into that room.'

If you're feeling devilish, you can hide an accomplice somewhere nearby whose job it is to jump out at a pre-arranged moment and shout something. Be warned, however, that this can traumatise people who are weak of heart.

KIDSKILL #5
BUILD A FORT

BUILDING A GOOD FORT will give you privacy, as well as a place to keep your stuff safe from grabby sibling hands.

THE GOAL:
To build a functioning fort that is complete with walls and an entrance, and that offers some degree of privacy – and earns you the envy of friends and family.

THE EQUIPMENT:
Indoor forts
- available space close to a bed, sofa or other piece of furniture
- thin blankets and/or old sheets
- pillows and cushions
- sturdy chairs
- big cardboard box
- scissors

Outdoor forts
- spot that is already partially 'built' (alongside a stone wall or fence, between two trees, next to a patch of thick bushes, etc.)
- tree branches
- old sheets

Don't build forts in hallways or other high-traffic areas. A fort should have a strategic location that is hard to reach, so putting it in the middle of the kitchen, for example, doesn't make sense.

THE SKILL:

'Building a Fort Indoors'

1 Pick an area out of the main flow of traffic but with at least one large piece of furniture (sofa, bed, table tennis table) to build against. Basements, playrooms and, if your parents are really easygoing, guest rooms are all good choices. You might mention to your parents that you want to temporarily rearrange part of the house. If you don't warn them, they may very well rearrange your pocket money from whatever it is now to nothing.

Even forts have fire codes. Don't set up a fort near a radiator, electronic equipment, lamp or fireplace. Never bring candles in or near a fort. You may, however, bring piping hot toast into a fort without fear.

2 This fort will be square. Nothing against rhombuses or decahedrons, but squares are just easier. The furniture will form one side and two corners of your fort. Place chairs where the two other corners will be.

Once you've mastered the art of building a square fort, you will be able to expand the size of your forts. They can be various shapes and can include multiple rooms.

3 To form the lower part of the walls, prop big, sturdy pillows or cushions between the bed or sofa and the chairs. Don't take any pillows from under a head that is sleeping at the time. If your home is low on cushions or pillows, opt for cardboard walls, cut from large boxes.

4 To make the roof, drape a blanket or sheet over the top of all the furniture. You might need to tie it or tuck it to make it secure. You can also let the roof hang down along the sides to form the top part of the walls.

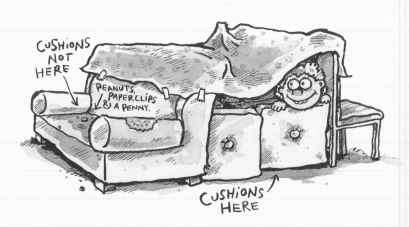

CUSHIONS NOT HERE

PEANUTS, PAPERCLIPS & A PENNY.

CUSHIONS HERE

If the ceiling sags, find something to place in the centre of the fort that is tall enough to keep it up, such as a long-legged stool or an unplugged floor lamp. Do not use your parents' favourite antiques! Do not even use some of their lesser-liked antiques.

5 Inside the fort, decorate as desired. Add more pillows or cushions as seats. If there's room, bring in small tables or boxes to act as tables. Other good fort accessories include a radio, books and snacks. Reality check: don't set up an appointment with the cable company to install television. As cool as your fort is, it is not a permanent residence.

You can make a multi-level fort if you have a bunk bed.

'Building a Fort Outdoors'

1 Scout out locations. If possible, choose a space that is already a bit secluded and surrounded by plants or rocks so you won't have to build every wall. You might even be able to find a ready-to-go fort that needs no additional construction at all! Look for good places near large stones or boulders, alongside fences or hedges, or under low-hanging trees or bushes.

2 Old garden furniture, such as folding chairs and picnic tables, makes excellent outdoor fort structures.

3 To form the walls and ceilings of your fort, drape old sheets between the trees, bushes, boulders or garden furniture.

4 Prop broken branches to hold up the ceiling if need be. (Use pre-broken branches. Don't snap them off the trees yourself!) Since you're outside, you can 'screw' the bottoms of the branches into the ground to anchor them.

5 If your parents don't need the sheets back, cut holes in them with scissors to form windows.

6 Name your fort and make a sign to hang or lean outside it. You can even make a fort flag, tape it to a stick and fly it with pride.

Don't cut out all four sides of the window. Leave the top side intact so that you are left with a flap you can lift when scouting for danger and lower when enemies approach.

LOOKOUT

OLD TABLE

KIDSKILL #6
HOST A GARDEN FÊTE

A SUMMER WITHOUT A FÊTE is like a fairground without rides – it just doesn't feel complete. Travelling fairs – you know, the kind where they unpack the big wheel from a little suitcase – visit different towns. While you're waiting for your town's Easter or summer fair to blow in, or if it's already left, build your own garden fête. No big wheel assembly – or disassembly – required.

THE GOAL:
To put together a simple garden fête and invite family, friends, and neighbours to come enjoy the activities.

THE EQUIPMENT:
- various activities and snacks, detailed below

Rather than surprise your parents with a back garden full of fête-goers, check with them first. Sell them the idea by predicting it will raise the property value on your garden – or at least make your family the most popular in the area!

There is no limit to what you can include in your fête, so long as it doesn't require a seat belt. You can take some, all, or none of the following suggestions, and add your own ideas based on what you like about fêtes.

THE SKILL:

1 Choose an evening for the fête.

2 Clean your garden or whatever space you will be using. Put away all tools, toys, garden gnomes, plastic flamingos and anything else that will not be a part of your fête.

3 Think of a name for your fête.

4 Develop your attractions. Here are some ideas.

Fish Fast. Make or buy waterproof fish with magnets attached. To make them, cut fish shapes out of cardboard, laminate them and glue on a magnet with waterproof glue. Make several fishing rods with sticks or rulers and strings (each piece cut to be about 1 metre long). Tie or glue a magnet to the end of each string. Fill a paddling pool with water and plop in the fish. Visitors who catch more than three fish in thirty seconds win a prize.

WATERPROOF (LAMINATED CARDBOARD) FISH WITH STEEL WASHERS FOR EYES!

YES, REAL FISH ARE ALREADY WATERPROOF BUT THEY DON'T STICK TO MAGNETS

Guess the Number. Count out a large number of some small item such as pennies or jelly beans. Fill a clear glass jar with them. Everyone who attends can write their guess and name on a slip of paper. Before you close the fête, go through the slips and award a prize to anyone who is correct. If no one is exactly right, give a prize for the closest guess.

Ready, Aim, Throw. Set up a throwing game. Line up a row of empty milk cartons (or something similar) on a table. Contestants must stand a certain distance away. Using tennis balls, they have four throws to knock all the cartons over. Anyone who does it gets a prize.

Test Your Balance. Pile a table with paperback books. Whoever can balance five books in each hand while walking back and forth for three minutes wins a prize.

5 Gather a bunch of small, cheap, but fun prizes – a packet of chewing gum, a pack of cards, a comic book, a box of crayons, a pair of flip-flops, a bag of balloons, a small puzzle, a magnet, a snack from your snack bar, a tube of lip balm and so on.

The easiest way to award prizes is to have a prize table. Give all game operators a stack of 'winner' coupons (design them on the computer and print them out). The game operators will give every winner a coupon that can be exchanged for one prize at the prize table.

6 Serve snacks such as muesli bars, apples and home-made biscuits. Price snacks in increments of twenty-five (25p, 50p, 75p, £1) so giving change is easier. Offer iced water and paper cups to help customers wash down the concessions. Ask local businesses if they'll donate food for the event in exchange for a little free publicity – offer to have stacks of their flyers, coupons or menus at your snack bar. Some may be willing to donate prizes, too.

7 Recruit trusted family and friends to stand by the entrance, the games, the prize table and the snack bar. Only the snack bar person will need to handle actual money. Make sure they have a cash box with change, especially 5p, 10p and 20p coins, and that they never let it out of their sight. (Make sure they're someone you can trust – greedy siblings might not be best for this job!)

8 Spread the word to family, friends, and neighbours by e-mail. You can also hang flyers in the area or post them through front doors. Include the name of the fête, the date(s), the location and the hours of operation.

9 Decorate the garden any way you'd like. Maybe all it needs is a string of coloured Christmas lights, plugged in by an extension cord and draped over the climbing frame.

Don't charge an admission fee. Instead, have a donation bucket at the entrance and let each visitor decide how much to give. However, you may send out telepathic messages to people as they walk in: £20, £50, £100 ... (If your main summer goal is to earn money, the fête is probably not for you. The best way to do this is raising money for your school or a charity.)

10 Set out rubbish bins, clearly labelled 'litter', in several different places.

11 If you know any musicians, ask if they'd like to play at your fête. If not, and you want music, place speakers in the windows of your house and pipe music out.

For safety and security, make your house off-limits to guests. Most people who come probably live close enough to run home to their own bathrooms!

KIDSKILL #7
WRITE/DIRECT/PERFORM A PLAY

NO KID WANTS TO WATCH STALE SITCOM RE-RUNS all summer, especially if you suspect you might be just as (or more) talented than the people you see on TV. So why not prove it by putting on your own summer production? Hollywood might come calling . . .

Summer theatre is most fun when performed outdoors, but you'll need to have a rain date. Unless, of course, you're putting on an adaptation of the story of Noah's ark.

THE GOAL:
To create a short play, and stage it in your back garden for family, friends and neighbours.

THE EQUIPMENT:
- computer (on which to write the play and make flyers)
- access to a photocopier (to make copies of the play for the actors)
- actors
- space to perform (any back garden will do nicely)
- costumes as needed
- props as needed

If any of your chosen actors seem reluctant, tell them that you're disappointed because now you'll have to ask your second choice. Then casually name some hot celebrity. Try to pick a celeb that resembles your actor at least a little bit.

THE SKILL:

1 Write the play. It can be about anything you want and should be less than forty-five minutes long. Have roles for boys and girls (or parts either could play, like animals or robots). Give it a beginning, a middle and an end, plus some kind of conflict or problem that gets solved.

If you're stumped for a plot, pick a story you already know (a book or film you loved will be fine) and 'adapt' it by rewriting the story as a play.

2 Cast the play. There are two ways to do this:

Hold real auditions. Pick a scene from your play and ask each actor who wants to try out to read the scene.

Ask family and friends to be the actors. Tell each of them that you wrote a certain role with them in mind.

3 Establish a rehearsal schedule and ask people to stick to it. Bribe them with food or sweets if necessary.

Make rehearsals fun, not work, or your actors might throw a tantrum and walk away, leaving you to perform the play as a one-person show. If you can't stop yourself from being a control freak, or you're just bursting with talent, make it a solo show from the start.

4 Gather or make any costumes and props you will need. Be creative – many an excellent wig has been made from a mop head and many a kid has become elderly thanks to talcum powder and eyeliner.

5 Before the première of your play, send an invitation by snail mail or e-mail to family and friends or put up flyers.

6 Welcome your audience and introduce the play. Then watch what you created come to life.

You can charge for admission, but you'll almost certainly have a better turnout if you make it free. If you do charge for admission, keep it cheap – after all, those re-runs are free. If you are really organised, you can make cakes and biscuits to sell at the interval and earn some cash off the theatre bar.

ALAS, POOR YORICK...

KIDSKILL #8
MAKE YOUR OWN
BLOCKBUSTER

THIS SUMMER, instead of being only on the viewing end of a blockbuster, be on the creating end as well.

THE GOAL:
To make a film that could qualify as a summer blockbuster – if only you had a bigger budget.

THE EQUIPMENT:
- computer (on which to write the movie script and create flyers)
- access to a photocopier (to make copies of the script for the actors)
- actors
- costumes as needed
- props as needed
- stiff card
- marker
- camcorder
- camcorder cassettes
- editing equipment (optional)

On second thought, don't obsess about budget. You don't need eye-popping special effects, fourteen locations and a hit theme song to make a film a true blockbuster. You only need to tell a great story.

Always ask before filming on private property, and even public property if your filming may interfere with other people's activities. You don't want your grumpy next-door neighbour unleashing his blood-sucking cocker spaniel on you when he finds you filming in his garden.

32

THE SKILL:

1 For writing and casting the film, see steps 1 and 2 of How to Write/Direct/Perform a Play. The only exception to this: if your old neighbour or mum's second cousin's wife younger brother happens to be a real celeb. Call and ask them to star — or else you'll tell the tabloids about the night they wet his pants after being freaked out by the ferocious sound of…a fox snuffling around outside.

2 Select your locations. Try to use existing and convenient locations. Example: say one of your scenes takes place on the moon. Problem is, you don't exactly have access to a rocket. Solution: find a dusty patch of land, one without vegetation or buildings in the background. Voila! Instant moonscape.

3 Once your script and actors are ready to go, decide how you will film. Ask your actors if they would rather rehearse their scenes or just learn their lines and actions before each shot. If they want to rehearse, make a schedule.

Unless you have access to editing equipment and know-how to use it, you will need to shoot the scenes of your film in order.

4 If you don't have digital editing equipment that allows you to type in titles and credits, write your film's title and credits on a piece of stiff card. Film the title card and credits cards. (You can get creative with this; spell out the title using ABC refrigerator magnets or pasta shapes – anything related to the theme or look of your blockbuster.)

5 Block and film your first scene. If somebody messes up or something goes wrong, rewind the tape and re-shoot over it. Do this as many times as you want. Don't move on to the next scene until you're happy with the current one.

Since you probably don't have any professional stunt people on the set, use action figures for your big stunts – they can't complain and they won't get hurt.

6 Continue filming each scene. If special effects are called for, have a brainstorming session with cast and crew before the shot. Someone may come up with an ingenious and totally doable solution.

SPECIAL EFFECTS ON THE CHEAP!

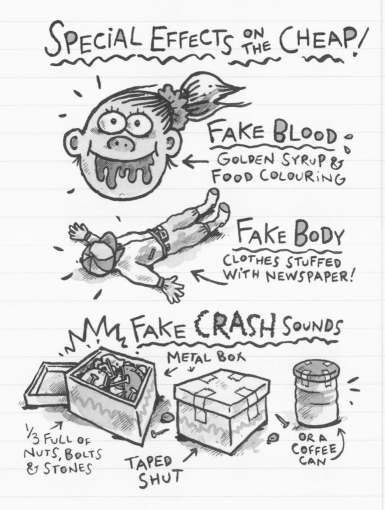

FAKE BLOOD ← GOLDEN SYRUP & FOOD COLOURING

FAKE BODY ← CLOTHES STUFFED WITH NEWSPAPER!

FAKE CRASH SOUNDS

METAL BOX

1/3 FULL OF NUTS, BOLTS & STONES

TAPED SHUT

OR A COFFEE CAN

7 When the film is completed, set up a screening. Invite family and friends. Serve popcorn. Dim the lights. Sit back and relax. Turn off all mobile phones and pagers. Enjoy the show!

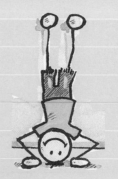

TRiCK
SKiLLZ

KIDSKILL #9
HAVE A SNOWBALL FIGHT IN JULY

TO DO THIS, you need to prepare in advance — way in advance. But it'll be worth it when you're zapping your pals with real snowballs in July.

If it never snows where you live, you may have to ask a friend who lives in a more northerly place to ship you some snowballs packed in a cooler overnight.

THE GOAL:
To make snowballs in winter, store them in a freezer, then take them out in summer and have a unique snowball fight.

THE EQUIPMENT:
- snow
- bucket
- freezer
- cool box(es)
- ice
- patient parents
- plastic freezer bags or baking sheets (optional)

You'll need to take over substantial space in the freezer and your parents may not be crazy about that if it means less room for leftover lasagne and frozen pies. An extra freezer would be a good thing.

THE SKILL:

1 Before the next snowstorm, clear out a section of the freezer or, better yet, a whole freezer if your family has an extra one. It doesn't have to be empty, but the more space you have, the more snowballs you can preserve.

2 After a snowfall, make as many snowballs as you can. Transport the snowballs in a bucket to the freezer. You may need to put each snowball in its own plastic freezer bag so all the snowballs don't freeze into one giant snow mound.

BE PREPARED EARLY

FREEZER FULL OF SNOWBALLS!

Don't use muddy snow, and definitely don't use yellow snow.

SEAL IN THE FRESHNESS

Ask friends to make and save their own snowballs.

3 Save your snowballs for a scorcher of a day. Invite your friends over and get them to bring their own snowballs.

4 Place the cool boxes around the garden – in the shade whenever possible. Spread them out so there will be accessible cool boxes in many spots during the fight.

As winter turns to spring, your parents may get tired of the lack of freezer space. They might tell themselves that you have forgotten your snowballs. At least once a week, mention how much you're looking forward to your summer snowball showdown.

THEN... WHEN SUMMER COMES...

5 If the snowballs are closer to iceballs, leave the lid open to let them soften a bit before starting. You don't want to hurt anyone so never start play until the snowballs are safely slushy. Then you're ready for some cool summer fun!

6 On the count of three, everyone run to a cool box, grab a snowball, aim and throw.

Never aim for anyone's head (and avoid the windows, especially if you want to stay on your parents' good side.)

The heat will melt the snowballs very quickly, so get everything organised in advance, then make the most of your snowball time!

BUCKET THAT USED TO BE FULL OF SNOWBALLS.

KIDSKILL #10
PERFORM AN AMAZING CARD TRICK

KIDS WHO CAN PULL OFF A CARD TRICK belong to an exclusive club. It takes a fast hand and a devious mind...

The more entertaining your delivery, the less likely the audience will figure out any of your tricks. If you're not confident in your ability to do this, plant a friend or two in the audience to act massively impressed at your sleights of hand. (Is that cheating? Well, what card trick isn't?)

THE GOAL:
To perform a card trick that makes jaws drop and eyes widen, preferably at the same time. You will know you've succeeded beyond expectations if spectators say, 'How'd you *do* that?' (Or, a little more embarrassingly, 'How'd *you* do that?').

THE EQUIPMENT:
- full pack of cards (fifty-two total)
- table
- eager audience, including potential volunteers
- top hat and cape (optional; for effect only)

A true magician does not reveal how they do it. Resist the urge to tell all, no matter how desperately your audience begs for it. Ultimately, you will be respected more if you maintain the mystery.

THE SKILL:

In this trick called 'Four Friendly Kings', you will unite all four kings in the pack after the audience has watched you separate them.

Before you're in front of the audience:

1 Gather the four king cards.

2 Put one king on the top of the pack (with the cards facing down).

KING ON TOP

3 Fan out the other three kings in your hand and hide one other card (any card except that king from the top of the pack) behind the middle king. Critical: Line up the secret card exactly with the middle king so the audience cannot see it.

SECRET CARD BEHIND THIS KING

With the audience:

4 Tell the audience that there is a land where four kings are best friends. After one king disappears in the woods (the pack of cards), the other three bravely set out to find him.

5 Show the audience the three kings in fan formation – again, only after you're sure the secret card is undetectable behind the middle king. Then close the fan. (In magician lingo, this is called 'squaring' the cards.)

41

6 Put those four cards on top of the pack, facing down (the same direction as the cards in the pack).

7 Explain that the three kings decide the best search strategy is to split up.

8 The first king journeys to the far end of the forest. From the top of the pack, take the first card (which is a king) and put it on the bottom of the pack.

9 The second king heads to the centre of the forest. From the top of the pack, take the second card (which is NOT a king) and put it in the middle of the pack. Make sure no one sees the face of this card as you move it.

10 The third king waits at the entrance to the forest. Leave the third card (which is a king) on the top of the pack. (The audience does not realise you are secretly leaving another king there with him, the one that you put there before you started the trick.)

You can show the audience the first King card as you move it, but this is risky, because they then may ask to see the second card you move, which would ruin the trick, of course, since it's not really a King. Size up your audience and use your best judgement.

IN ACTUALITY

REST OF PACK →

← KING
← KING
← KING

↑ KING

11 Explain that since this is happening long before mobile phones were invented, the kings have agreed to meet at a certain spot in one hour to touch base. Cut the pack, putting the bottom half of the pack on to the top. Do this by moving your arm in a clockwise motion and finish by saying, 'The hour's up'.

12 Search through the pack to show where the three kings have rendezvoused – and to reveal that they found the missing fourth king, too!

CUT PACK & PUT BOTTOM HALF ON TOP OF TOP HALF! (THIS PUTS ALL FOUR KINGS TOGETHER & IN THE MIDDLE!)

KIDSKILL #11
MAKE A COIN DISAPPEAR

WHEN YOUR GRANDPA first pulled a penny out from behind
your ear, you probably thought you'd be a millionaire. By now,
you know that there's no cash stashed behind anyone's hearing
organs . . . but you can make other people think there is.

Unfortunately, money does not grow on trees (or behind ears). You have to earn it first — or borrow it — for this trick.

THE GOAL:

To make a coin disappear from your hand and reappear behind
the ear of an audience member.

THE EQUIPMENT:

- coin (whichever one fits most comfortably in your hand)
- your hand
- someone else's ear (still attached, please)

THE SKILL:

1 Hold a coin between the thumb and
forefinger of your right hand, palm
up. Show the coin to the audience
along with your left hand, which
should be wide open. Turn both
hands over to show that you have
'nothing up your sleeve'. (Note: Do this
even if you are wearing a sleeveless shirt.)

AUDIENCE

44

If you are left-handed, congratulations! (Lefties are known to be very creative kids.) Oh, and just reverse the hand directions in these steps.

WHAT THEY SEE ←

2 Still holding the coin between the thumb and forefinger of your right hand, bring your left hand over to your right as if you were going to grab the coin with it. At the same time, subtly curl the bottom three fingers of your right hand into your palm to form a small cup.

3 Pass your left hand over the coin and pretend to snatch it. At the same time, release the coin into your cupped right hand.

4 Immediately close your left hand tightly to indicate that you are holding the coin there.

5 Try to hold your right hand as casually as possible. Use the index finger and thumb of your right hand to point to the coin in your left hand, all the while palming the coin in your right hand.

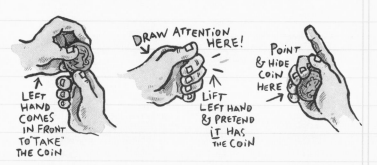

LEFT HAND COMES IN FRONT TO "TAKE" THE COIN

DRAW ATTENTION HERE!

LIFT LEFT HAND & PRETEND IT HAS THE COIN

POINT & HIDE COIN HERE

6 You're ready to make the coin disappear. Bring your left hand to your mouth and blow on it. Open that hand to reveal that the coin is 'no longer' there. Remember to keep your right hand as loose as possible.

Let the audience 'ooh' and 'aah', but not for too long. They may start looking around for the coin and notice your oddly 'cramped' right hand.

7 Announce that you're about to make the coin reappear and that you suspect it is somewhere on someone in the audience.

8 If you have a small audience, walk among them, pretending to search everyone's head as if you're not sure where the coin went. If you have a larger audience, act as though you know on whom the coin is, but not where on his body. Call that person up to the front.

9 Once you've singled out the coin's 'host', pretend you see something behind his ear. With your right hand, reach behind that ear.

AHA!

10 Let the coin fall forwards to your fingertips as you bring your hand forwards. The audience will think you pulled it out of his ear.

KIDSKILL #12
STAND ON YOUR HEAD/
DO A HANDSTAND

Being upside down is one of life's great pleasures that, for some reason, only kids can appreciate. It gives you a unique perspective and makes everyone else look really weird. If you can actually walk on your hands, you get super stunt-kid status.

Don't practise headstands or handstands on hard surfaces. You will definitely take a few falls while you are learning, and it's much nicer (and safer) to land on a soft surface such as a lawn — or at least a rug.

THE GOAL:

'Headstand' To balance on your head (and hands).

'Handstand' To balance upside down on just your hands.

THE EQUIPMENT:
- your hands
- your head
- a wall
- flat, soft surface
- cushion or folded-up blanket (optional)

THE SKILL:

'The Headstand'

Don't let all your weight bear down on your bonce. Spread it out over your hands, too.

1 Pick a spot about a hand's length away from your wall. Kneel down and put the very top of your head on the ground and place your hands about shoulder-width apart on either side of your head.

2 Lift your knees off the floor and stick your bum as high in the air as it can go with your feet still on the ground. Now kick one leg into the air, followed immediately by the other, so that they're parallel to the wall. It's okay if your feet hit the wall, but don't rest them there – that's cheating.

3 Bring your feet away from the wall so you are balancing without help. Keep your back and legs straight and strong. Try to hold your position for ten seconds.

4 When you're ready to come down, just lower one leg at a time back down in front of your face, then slowly sit back on to your knees. Try to control the movement. It kind of ruins the effect if you fall out of a headstand.

Make sure you have nothing embarrassing in your pockets because you never know what might fall out. Oh, yeah – and tuck your shirt in!

'The Handstand'

1 Now that you know you can balance on your head and hands, it's time to take your head out of the game and see if you can do a handstand. Once again, you're going to need that wall. Put both hands on the floor about a hand's length away from the wall.

2 Stick your bum high in the air. Kick up with one leg, then the other. It's okay to hit the wall — use it for support.

3 Once you're up and you're not too wobbly, remove your legs from the wall, one at a time, and balance. Try to keep your body as straight as a board. Squeeze your thighs together and tighten your stomach muscles. If you arch your back or bend at the hips, gravity will pull you down.

4 Come down one leg at a time, slowly.

If you feel like you're going to fall and you can't come down one leg at a time, try to bail out with some dignity by tucking your head and rolling into a somersault. (You can't be near the wall, though.) Imagine you're Jackie Chan and let people think you did it on purpose.

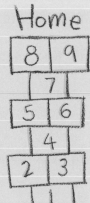

Home

8	9
	7
5	6
	4
2	3
	1

GAME
Skillz

KIDSKILL #13
PLAY CAPTURE THE FLAG

WITH ALMOST NO EFFORT, any back garden or park can be converted into the site of an epic confrontation. Capture the Flag is a fast-paced game that requires stealth, strategy and stamina – and worthy opponents.

THE GOALS:
To strategise with your team, fan out and hunt down the opposing team's hidden flag.

This game is high–energy but low–maintenance. You need nothing more than two flags, which can be made from something as simple as a T–shirt or a duster.

THE EQUIPMENT:
- two teams of at least three people each
- two different-coloured flags (they can be any kind of cloth, but should be a similar size)
- terrain on which to play
- unlimited energy
- cunning

Set aside a whole afternoon for Capture the Flag. A game with two clever, evenly matched teams can last a while.

THE SKILL:

1 Divide your players into two even teams – even in both number and ability. Don't put all the speed demons on one team and the daydreamers on the other.

2 Decide on the course. Each team will have an equal-size territory (home base, headquarters or whatever you want to call it) in which to hide and guard its flag. You can play small scale (one team gets the front garden, the other the back) or big (opposite ends of a park) – but not too big (opposite ends of the galaxy). Establish boundaries so players aren't wandering too far.

3 Each team decides who will take what role.

Assign one person to guard the flag. This is the only player who is sure to encounter others in the game, so they should be a person who has no fear of confrontation – or of flags, come to think of it.

Assign one person to guard the jail (more on the jail below). This should be a person who likes standing around.

The rest of the players can be either attacking (going after the other team's flag) or defensive (patrolling their team's territory to intercept members of the opposing team).

Even before the game officially begins, secret agents can be dispatched to spy out the other side's setup and possibly even learn where its flag is hidden before things get started. If you do this, however, tread carefully. Spies who are caught are rarely invited to play again, although everyone silently agrees that they're wickedly cool.

GOOD GUARD

NOT-so-GOOD GUARD

GHOUL'S GYM

4 Both teams have five minutes to hide their flags somewhere in their territory.

Each flag must be visible from at least one angle from a distance of about 3 metres. That means that you can hide it behind a tree but cannot bury it beneath a tree.

It cannot be tied or otherwise secured to anything – a player must be able to grab it quickly.

It must stay in one place during the whole game and therefore cannot be held by a player (unless, of course, an opposing team member is grabbing it and running with it).

You can't hide decoy flags.

5 Each team calls out when its flag is hidden. Then the game starts.

6 Attacking players begin their attempts to discover and take the opposing team's flag. This will ultimately involve distracting, sneaking past or jailing the guard of the flag.

7 Any player can be 'caught' by another player by being tagged.

An alternative way to catch opposing players is by using swatches of cloth. Each player tucks an equal-sized swatch of cloth into their belt or the top of their jeans so the cloth dangles down their leg. The swatch can't be tucked in too tight as it must come loose with one tug. It also can't be hidden under clothing but must be visible. If another player snags your cloth, you're caught. However, if another player accidentally snags your belt and your shorts fall down, you're embarrassed but not caught.

* HiNT: iF YOU CAN'T FiND A SWATCH, USE YOUR UNDERWEAR. i BET NOBODY WiLL WANT TO CATCH YOU...

8 When a player is tagged or their swatch is snagged, they must report to the opposing team's jail. The jail is simply a place where captured players must stand until they're rescued or the game ends. In other words, you won't have to eat gruel or sleep in a dungeon or anything like that. A player sent to jail remains there unless a fellow team member frees them. Anyone can free jailed team members by touching them and shouting 'Jailbreak!' Once free, they must return directly to their team's territory before starting to play again, and they can't be recaptured as they return there. However, the person who started the jailbreak can be captured at any point in the process.

If four team members are jailed but the jailbreaker has time to touch only two before running off, only those two can escape.

9 If a player captures a flag but is tagged before reaching their side, they go to jail and the flag is returned to its hiding place. However, if they pass the flag to a fellow team member before getting tagged, the flag is still in play.

10 The game ends when one team captures the opposing team's flag and is able to take it to its own side without being caught.

If the game ends before either flag is captured, the team that has jailed the most players from the opposing team wins.

KIDSKILL #14
PLAY HOPSCOTCH

KIDS HAVE BEEN PLAYING HOPSCOTCH for more than 2,000 years – really! – so if you don't want to mess up a long tradition, you should play at least once before you grow up.

THE GOAL:
To throw a stone with perfect aim and hop better, faster and longer than any other hopscotchers in your street.

THE EQUIPMENT:
- chalk
- marker such as a coin, pebble, or other small object
- flat, hard surface
- shoes comfortable for hopping

When hopscotch was invented (by soldiers in ancient Rome), there were no cars to run over the players. But since your neighbourhood does have cars, stay on the pavement or in your driveway.

THE SKILL:

1 Get at least one friend to play, but more than two is fine.

2 Draw a hopscotch board on asphalt or use the paving stones as squares.

3 The first player tosses their marker into square 1. It must land completely within the intended square, or it's the next player's turn.

4 The first player hops up the board, starting with square 1. The player hops on the single squares with one foot and the side-by-side squares with both feet.

56

There is a good reason to use chalk instead of something more permanent like paint: chalk washes off. Though you might like a permanent hopscotch game in front of your house, chances are your parents won't. There's a little something called house prices that adults get very worked up over.

5 Upon reaching the top of the board, the player turns and hops back down the board in the same way. The player must pick up their marker on the way back, ideally by scooping it up as they go.

6 If the player finishes the board successfully, they go again by tossing their marker into square 2 and repeating the hopping sequence. Stop playing when you start to feel like an oversize rabbit.

If a player steps on a line, misses a square or loses their balance, it's the next player's turn. The first player starts their next turn where they goofed on their last turn.

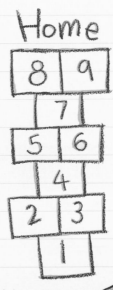

KIDSKILL #15
PLAY SKULLY

SKULLY MAY SOUND LIKE a game that pirates used to play in between looting coastal villages, but it probably started in the U.S. on the streets of New York in the 1930s. A good skully player (aka 'killer diller') can achieve legendary status among the kids in – and even beyond – their own street.

THE GOAL:
To be the envy of every other skully player in the neighbourhood by having better aim.

THE EQUIPMENT:
- chalk
- bottle caps
- flat, hard surface
- good aim
- ruthlessness

So what if you've never heard of this game? There was a time when you'd never heard of pizza, but that didn't stop you from getting all addicted to it, did it?

THE SKILL:

1 Round up at least two friends, up to as many as you want. You can play against enemies, too.

2 With chalk, plot out the skully board on asphalt.

Don't worry if your spacing is not exact or your lines are a little crooked. You can always blame it on the uneven surface you have to write on.

58

3 Each player arms themselves with a bottle cap. It is ideal if each player's cap is different from the other players' caps. For example, you can each use the caps from a different kind of bottled water or juice.

4 One at a time, each player places their cap at the start line. Take turns using your fingers to flick the bottle cap across the ground towards the 1-square (called 'the ones'). The first player whose bottle cap stops completely within the ones (on the line doesn't count) continues. Before flicking it again, they may position their cap within the 1-square anywhere they want – or leave it where it is.

5 The same player now flicks their bottle cap out of the ones towards the 2-square ('twos'). If they get it in on the first flick, they continue. If not, their turn is over, and the next player flicks towards the ones.

The squares around the 13-square are called 'the skull', which is where the game gets its name. The squares around the skull are called 'no man's land', or 'dead zone' or some other dread-inspiring name.

6 The game continues with each player moving through the board in sequence. When a player reaches the 13-square, they start shooting 'backwards', that is back down through the numbers to the 1-square, then once more into the 13. The winner is the one who gets back into the 13 first.

You can become a 'killer' after getting back from 13 by shooting your cap into all four 'dead zone' squares.

7 And if that isn't challenging enough, there are a few other tricky factors in skully.

You can flick your cap and knock another player's cap off of a square (on purpose or accidentally). If that happens, the player cannot move ahead until they shoot their cap into that square again, but you get to skip ahead one square.

The dead zone. If any player's cap comes to rest in the dead zone, their turn stops and they miss up to three turns or until another player knocks them out (by accident, of course). Skully has many variations. Modify the rules if you'd like, and you don't need to ask anyone's permission first. Just like a true pirate.

You can make up your own name for this zone, something that sends a shiver through your whole body, such as Kitty litter tray or school cafeteria.

KIDSKILL #16

BE AN EXPERT AT JACKS

JACKS MAY SEEM LIKE a little kid's game but it takes real co-ordination. An ace jacks player has lightning-quick reflexes and laser-sharp eye-hand co-ordination and can snatch small objects up in the blink of an eye. These skills can be useful in all sorts of ways . . .

THE GOAL:

To trounce the other players by throwing a ball up, then grabbing more jacks than anyone else before the ball bounces.

You do not have to be named Jack or Jacqueline to enjoy jacks, and being named Jack does not improve your chance of winning. But if that is your name, you can let on to the contrary to psych out your opponents.

THE EQUIPMENT:

- ten jacks
- small rubber ball (red suggested but not mandatory)
- flat, hard surface
- competitive spirit

Do not bluff and enter the jacks arena without skill. You will be exposed and taste a bitter defeat. Fortunately, this is a game you can practise by yourself.

THE SKILL:

1 Gather between one and five friends. Lure them by explaining they're about to enter the wild world of non-digital games.

2 Decide if you want to play on the ground or a table. If there are only two of you, face each other. If more than two, arrange yourselves in a circle. If you opt to play on a table, standing is recommended over sitting for maximum mobility.

One of the techniques for deciding who gets to play first also serves as a good warm-up. One at a time, each player throws all the jacks in the air and tries to catch as many as possible with both hands together, thumb to thumb, palms down. Whoever catches the most gets the honour.

3 Lightly scatter the ten jacks on to the playing surface. They should all fall within a reasonably sized imaginary circle. If any land in the next county, your circle is too big.

4 Toss the ball into the air with your throwing hand. With a little experience, you will work out a height that works best for you.

5 While the ball is airborne, pick up one jack (onesies), also with your throwing hand.

6 Catch the ball — again in your throwing hand — before it bounces. (The jack will still be in your hand.)

7 Now do it again, only pick up two jacks (twosies) before the ball bounces. Keep going till you've picked up all ten jacks. However, it's the next player's turn if any of the following happen:

you miss a jack

you miss the ball

you drop the jack(s), the ball or both

you don't pick up the correct number of jacks

When it's your turn again, begin where you left off. If you messed up when trying to pick up six jacks, start by going for six again.

8 The first person to scoop up all ten earns the right to do a brief victory dance of their choosing, but not too showy, please.

One variation is to bounce the ball on the playing surface instead of tossing it in the air, then try to snatch up as many jacks as you can before the ball bounces again. You can twist the game in other ways to suit you, too. One thing, however, should not be changed: jacks is a one-handed game. Resist creating any version where you can use both hands.

WATER
SKiLLZ

KIDSKILL #17
BE A MASTER STONE SKIMMER

Small stones must be meant for skimming because they certainly don't seem to be good for much else. And why else would there be so many of them alongside lakes and rivers? Skimming (sometimes called skipping) stones may seem simple enough, but there are ways you can improve your chances of increasing the number of bounces.

You might be accused of having stones for brains if you try to skim stones where people are swimming or boating. Skim only in unpopulated waters.

THE GOAL:
To throw a stone at the water so that it skims over the surface, bouncing at least three – but hopefully more – times.

THE EQUIPMENT:
- supply of small, flattish stones (look for stones with smooth edges)
- body of water (not too wavy is preferred but not essential)
- skim log (optional, to keep track of the number of bounces per toss)
- camcorder (optional but desirable to later give visual proof of a jaw-dropping feat)

Stones are ideal for this activity since they're easy to find (and afford), but you can try skimming other small, flat objects as well, such as shells or pieces of bark. Don't use anything that doesn't belong in the water naturally, like a paint-can lid or your brother's favourite DVD.

THE SKILL:

1 Wait for a clear day. If you skim when it's foggy or hazy, you may not see how many times your stone bounces.

Of course, if you think your stone-skimming talent will be underwhelming, poor visibility can work to your advantage. Later, just say something like, 'A guy on the other side of the pond saw my stone bounce 14 more times after it passed through that patch of fog'.

2 Stand at the shore of a lake, pond, river or even the sea if you're a daredevil. Gather family and friends if you like – competitive stone skimming needs witnesses.

3 Choose your stone. Look for the following characteristics:

uniform width – it should be the same thickness or thinness all over, but fairly flat

palm-size – small enough to grasp, big enough to watch as it flies over the water

shaped more like a triangle rather than a circle – these tend to bounce better

not too heavy – you need to toss it without difficulty

4 Position yourself at the water's edge.

NICE SIZE & SHAPE!

You don't have to skim competitively.
Some people find stone skimming peaceful.
You can do it while pondering life's deepest
mysteries or possibly just your next snack.

5 Hold the stone horizontally between your thumb and middle finger, with your thumb on top. Curl your index finger along the edge.

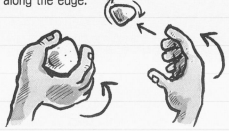

6 Face the water at a slight angle.

7 With your hand parallel to the water, cock your wrist and quickly flick the stone at the water, out and down at the same time. The lower your hand is when you release the stone, the better the results can be.

8 As you release the stone, the uncurling action of your index finger should add some spin to the throw. The spinning may help you achieve more bounces and it looks cool.

Three bounces are good. Six are awesome. More than ten would earn a gold medal if this were an Olympic sport. As of this writing, the world record for number of bounces in one throw is forty! If you beat that, contact the media.

KIDSKILL #18
PERFORM A SWAN DIVE/ JACKKNIFE/BACK DIVE

EVERY KID SHOULD be able to enter the water with style. Climbing down the ladder into a pool is not cool, so if you can master even one dive, you'll always be able to 'make a splash'.

As you probably know from all those signs around the local pool (or your cousin who got twenty-seven stitches in his head last summer), diving can be dangerous. Try these dives only when a lifeguard is on duty or an adult who can swim is present. Don't be put out about that – it just means you'll have more witnesses to your aerodynamic and aquatic grace. Also, do not practise diving without water.

THE GOAL:
To master the art of diving gracefully into the water with a swanlike arc, an athletic jackknife or a no-fear backwards dive.

THE EQUIPMENT:
- swimsuit or bathing trunks that won't fall off
- pool
- diving board (optional)
- friend who's a good photographer, to document your daring dives on film (optional)

THE SKILL:

Before performing any dive, inspect your performance area. Make sure the diving board is in good condition. Make sure the pool is clean. While you're at it, make sure the pool is filled with water.

'Swan Dive'

1 Stand at the pool end of the diving board, facing the water, arms at your sides.

2 Bend your knees, and pushing against the board with your feet, launch yourself off the board towards the water.

3 While airborne, keep your legs together, arch your back slightly and spread your arms sideways, making your body resemble a flying T. Or rather a flying swan.

4 As you approach the water, bring your arms together above your head to form a straight line with your body, keeping your head in line with your body. Enter the water that way. From that point on, you need not continue to imitate a swan.

This dive works really well from higher boards, since you have more time to move your arms from one position to the next while in the air. However, you can do it with no board if necessary but you might want to refer to the dive as your ugly duckling variation.

'Jackknife'

1 Stand near the pool end of the diving board, facing the water.

2 Launch yourself off the board towards the water.

3 While airborne, bend at the waist and touch your ankles without bending your knees.

4 Kick your legs up, straighten out and slice into the water smoothly, hands first.

5 Bask in the admiration of the crowd.

'Back Dive'

1 Stand near the edge of the deep end of the pool with your back to the water.

2 Lift your arms straight out in front of you as if you're a zombie. This will help you balance, though it's not known if this is why the undead do it.

3 With your feet parallel and about 3 cm apart, stand on the balls of your feet.

Skip the diving board for this one. It's daring enough to dive into the water when you can't actually see it — you don't need the extra height and bounce of a diving board.

4 Back one heel a smidgen over the edge of the pool, then the other. Balance is critical or else your back dive may turn into a back flop.

5 Lower your arms to your sides, then raise your arms in front of you again to a level slightly above your head. At the same time, push down with your toes.

6 To spring yourself off the pool edge, quickly drop your arms to your sides and bend your knees. Quickly swing your arms up again, past your face and over your head, and jump up and out, straightening your knees as you jump. This all happens faster than it took you to read this sentence.

7 As soon as you feel your feet leave solid ground, lift your legs so they point straight up, perpendicular to the water. Your head, meanwhile, will be pointing to the water.

8 Bring your arms up, keeping them in line with your body. Keep your whole body straight or else you won't enter the water correctly.

9 Pierce the water like an arrow shot straight down. Your hands should hit first.

With any dive, before exiting the pool, make sure your bathing suit is still on. If it's not, you may have to dive again right away but this time, to the bottom of the pool to retrieve it.

KIDSKILL #19
DO A CANNONBALL

IN PURELY TECHNICAL TERMS, a cannonball is less of a dive and
more of a jump – unlike a dive, it's not meant to be graceful.
You don't need to be an athlete to perform a spectacular
cannonball. Don't be fooled by its name – you do not need
a cannon to perform it and should not use one even if you
happen to have one. But the splash it makes when done
correctly is definitely explosive. If you are swimming in a
public pool, cannonballs and some other dives might not be
allowed so check the signs, or with your parents, first.

In the past, competitive cannonballing was dominated
by those who weighed the most. However, with a little
bit of strategy, even a seriously skinny kid can do a
memorable cannonball as it's about style as well as splash.

THE GOAL:
To enter the water with the largest splash range possible,
soaking everyone in the vicinity.

You may want to come up with your own
catchy phrase to yell during your
cannonball. Some that have worked for
people in the past include the following:

- 'Geronimo!'
- 'Timber!'
- 'Incoming!'
- 'Kowabunga!'
- 'Boo-yah!'

THE EQUIPMENT:

- swimsuit or trunks that won't fall off
- pool
- diving board (optional)
- friend who's a good photographer, to document your explosive jump on film (optional)

THE SKILL:

If possible, do this dive when there are dry people poolside. One mark of a successful cannonball is as many wet onlookers as possible.

1 Unlike most dives, this jump requires a major a run down the diving board. Pump those legs! The speed of your run is key to jumping high in the air.

2 When you get to the end, jump off the board as high into the air as you can. The height you reach is key to making a big splash.

3 While airborne, pull your legs up to your chest and wrap your arms around them, clasping them tight. You should now resemble a human cannonball.

4 Allow yourself to drop straight towards the water. If you're flexible enough to get one hand up to your face, use it to pinch your nose. As you near the water, hold your breath.

5 In your balled-up configuration, you should hit the water bum first, causing a huge splash (no matter how big your bum is). Some splashes spread out, others rocket up like a geyser. Both are acceptable.

KIDSKILL #20
DO A BELLY FLOP

DIVES CAN BE USED to make people gasp or laugh. If you'd rather amuse than amaze, this dive is for you. It doesn't take much agility or even practice BUT it may really hurt! However, it is guaranteed to attract the attention of everyone in and near the pool. If you've got the stomach for it, your belly flop may achieve legendary status.

The belly flop may not be elegant enough to be part of Olympic competition, but it deserves respect anyhow. You should perform it with pride. Any dive takes guts, particularly one where your gut goes first.

THE GOAL:
To enter the water flat on your belly, creating an enormous splash and eliciting admiring laughs, gasps and groans from onlookers.

THE EQUIPMENT:
- swimsuit or bathing trunks that won't fall off
- pool
- onlookers
- friend who's a good photographer, to document your delirious flop on film (optional)

This dive is the comical black sheep of the dive family, which means it is always the most captivating.

It is highly advisable to avoid this dive if you have recently eaten.

THE SKILL:

1 To eclipse all the other divers by making a large, uncomfortable splash. An audience is essential: If a person belly flops in the pool and nobody sees it, it may make a sound — but not a big impression.

2 You can start this dive from either a standing or running position.

3 For a classic, proud belly flop, as you reach your highest point, gloriously spread out your arms and legs so you look like a falling X. Then hold this position.

As with the cannonball, the belly flop need not be silent — in fact, shouting is an excellent enhancement.

4 For a comical variation, flail your arms and legs as if you're trying to get into a swan dive or jackknife position, making sure to get the maximum extension of arms and legs before you hit the water.

5 With either approach, you will hit the water belly first with a wince-inducing smack. Entering in the same position side-on may reduce the amount of pain you will suffer!

Don't belly flop from a diving board — go for drama, not height

NATURE
SKiLLZ

KIDSKILL #21
CLIMB A TREE

IF TREES WEREN'T MEANT TO BE CLIMBED, why would they have branches? Tree climbing is an essential kidskill – you can't graduate from kidhood unless you've done it. But first, ask your parents – you could even invite them to come and witness your tree-climbing prowess.

THE GOAL:
To get a bird's eye view of things from a tree.

THE EQUIPMENT:
- tree
- climbing shoes
- whistle
- gloves (optional)

If your parents think that climbing trees is dangerous, tell them that it is not climbing that is dangerous, but falling – and you don't plan to fall.

Not all trees are suitable for climbing. Avoid Christmas trees; trees in homes, offices and any tree skinnier than you are.

THE SKILL:

1 Gather your arbour armour. Put on the closest thing you have to climbing shoes. They should fit snugly and have traction (grip), since you'll want to get a good foothold with each step. Wear gloves if you think it will help you get a tighter grip, but not mittens.

2 Choose your tree wisely. You want a tree with nice, soft grass growing below it. It doesn't need to be high but make sure it is sturdy with no huge cracks in the trunk. Eyeball the branches. Do they look strong? Are they close enough together so you can reach each next one? Look for a tree with a thick branch low enough that you can reach it or, better yet, a V made by two joined branches.

Avoid trees with telephone or power lines running through them. You want a pure tree, untouched by human technology, the way nature intended it. Well, except if there's a wasps' nest up there.

3 Getting up on to the first branch is the biggest challenge. Find the lowest thick branch and wrap both arms around it. Now pull yourself up and on to it. Use your feet to push against the trunk to help you up. Or if you're feeling acrobatic, swing your feet up over the branch. If you can't reach it, even with jumping, pick another tree. Under no circumstances should you try to build a makeshift catapult to fling yourself up into a tree.

4 Once you're on the first branch, you're well on your way. Now you only have to repeat what you've already done – look for the next sturdy branch above and grasp it. Don't try for another branch until you're balanced. Tug down on every branch with one hand to test its strength before pulling yourself up. Some dead branches may be brittle and snap off.

You don't have to climb high or reach the top of the tree to prove your climbing skills. Climb until you reach a spot that's comfortable for you, even if it's only the second branch up. You'll still get some great views.

5 When you've reached your peak, find a fat branch to rest on and enjoy the new perspective. Feel free to yodel like Tarzan, whistle at passers-by or just stare at the clouds.

If you find that you can't get down, blow on your whistle or use your phone to call for help.

6 To descend, clasp the trunk with both hands and reach down carefully with one foot for the sturdy branch you used to climb up on. Going down may be a little harder since you will be looking at the ground more, which reminds you of how high up you are. So don't look down farther than the next branch. If you remember the way you came up, go down the same way since it's already proven to be a reliable path.

Don't rely on tree climbing to escape a charging bear. Bears can climb trees, too. Trees are, however, fine in the event of charging alligators.

KIDSKILL #22
DO A BIRD CALL

BIRDS MAKE A LOT OF NOISE, but you don't have to let them do all the talking. Speaking their language can come in handy whether you just want a closer look at them or you need to distract gullible adults. And bird language may be easier to learn than human language – at least you don't need to memorise irregular verbs.

THE GOAL:
To imitate the sounds of a bird so well that you can fool not only the people around you, but also the bird.

Bird calls or songs include lots of different, fun sounds, including hoots, chirps and trills. Learning to imitate them can greatly enlarge your repertoire of weird noises.

THE EQUIPMENT:
- birds
- your voice
- your ears
- your hands, in some cases
- breadcrumbs (optional)
- recording device of some kind (optional)
- pad and pen (optional)

A quick Internet search for bird call will bring up numerous sites that play the actual cheeps and peeps of birds worldwide. If you're having trouble hearing a bird outside, listen online in the meantime. But don't grow too fond of this convenience. Nothing compares to getting outside and listening in on the real squeal.

THE SKILL:

1 Go to a location that birds frequent. Parks are a good bet, as is your own back garden, especially if you have a bird table or birdbath there. When in doubt, look for bird poo, a clear sign of a bird hangout.

> If birds are scarce in your neighbourhood, try a local zoo.

2 To attract birds, try sprinkling a few breadcrumbs on the ground.

3 Once birds arrive, pay close attention to their sounds. You may have to wait awhile, but try not to get frustrated. (If only someone could translate 'Please chirp now' into bird talk . . .)

> Real bird-watchers often record the bird noises on a tape recorder or digital voice recorder. You could also simply write down the sounds you're hearing. Then you can practise long after the birds have flown to parts unknown.

4 As the birds chat away, try to reproduce the sounds you're hearing using your own lips, cheeks, fingers and vocal cords. Try making squeaks, whistles, kissy sounds and high-pitched sshhh's. If you're lucky, the birds will mistake you for one of their own and answer. (Just don't let a mother bird confuse you with her young – she might try to regurgitate a worm into your mouth.)

Another method is to put your palms together so your thumbs line up. Bend your hands slightly so there's a gap between the palms. Lock your fingers together. Wet your lips. Press them on your thumbs, bottom lip on the knuckles, top lip on your fingernails. Blow lightly.

5 Here are some interpretations of the sounds of certain common birds. Keep in mind that this is an inexact science. What sounds like a hoot to you may sound like a twoot to someone else.

Blackbird: chook pink pink pink

Canada goose: honk honk honk

Coot: kowk kowk kekowk

Duck mallard/teal: quack/cric cric

Herring gull: kyow kyow kyowww kyok

Robin: tic tic-ic tic tic-ic

Starling: cher tic tic peuw

Woodpigeon: cu-coooo cu-coooo

KIDSKILL #23
CAMP OUT IN YOUR GARDEN

A SUMMER NIGHT, you're lying on your back, staring up at the sky . . . but wait, why are you looking at your bedroom ceiling? Even if your parents would rather be eaten by red ants than take you camping, you can still sleep under the stars – simply do it in your own back garden.

CITY KIDS: you may not have a safe garden, or any garden! If your back garden is a back alley, don't cuddle up to dustbins or iron railings. You'll need to venture out to a grassy area to enjoy this activity. Perhaps you have a friend in the suburbs who will lend you a patch of lawn for one night. Always tell a parent before camping in the garden and never camp in a public park.

THE GOAL:
To spend a whole night eating, talking and sleeping in nature, even if it's only the nature of your back garden.

If you decide to camp out in your back garden, act as though you really are deep in the forest. Bring everything you'd need if your house weren't right there. Do NOT go back into the house for any reason (except illness or grave danger). Nothing deflates the mood of a camping night like running back into the house before bedding down to check your e-mail or catch a re-run of your favourite sitcom.

THE EQUIPMENT:

- tent
- sleeping bag
- camping buddy (optional)
- plastic bottle with water
- insect repellant
- sweatshirt and tracksuit bottoms
- torch
- nature-friendly entertainment (book, pack of cards, pad and paper to sketch or write, transistor radio, etc.)
- snacks

WHAT NOT TO TAKE:
- *mobile phone*
- *laptop computer*
- *handheld video game (come on, give nature a chance)*

THE SKILL:

1 Pick a date. Check the weather to help you decide on a night for your camping trip. Since no hike is required and no fire-building is allowed, you can actually consider doing it on a rainy night. No, you're not allergic to rain. In fact, some drizzle might make the experience more memorable.

2 Assemble your gear.

3 Choose a spot as far from the house as you can.

4 In the afternoon, head out to your location and set up your tent. Depending on how handy you are, allow anywhere from five minutes to several hours for this task – some tents are complicated (since your parents are going to know all about this expedition, you might as well ask for help, too).

5 Eat your tea as the sun sets.

6 After eating, relax in front of the tent. Chat, tell ghost stories, read by torchlight or just listen to the sounds of the evening. Get some exercise by flicking away mosquitoes that are undeterred by your repellant spray.

You can go it alone or invite friends. If neighbourhood friends can't stay over but know what you're doing, they may try to play a prank on you or scare you. Be ready with some revenge pranks of your own.

The one exception to the 'don't go in the house' rule: the bathroom. It's probably best if you take advantage of modern plumbing rather than make a mess on the lawn that will still be there in the morning. (While you're inside, you might as well brush your teeth, too.)

7 When it gets really dark, stargaze for a while. If you're lucky, you'll spot a shooting star.

8 Hit the sack not when your watch indicates it's your usual bedtime but when you feel like it. You may find that it will be earlier than usual since you don't have your everyday distractions (TV, computer, phone), or you may find the fresh air and new experience energise you, inspiring you to stay up late into the night.

Ask your family to work with you if they're not participating in your camping expedition. Request that they leave house lights off as much as possible so as not to pollute your camping environment. Tell them not to disturb you with phone calls, quick questions and most importantly, chores.

KIDSKILL #24
HATCH A PEACOCK BUTTERFLY

MOST BUTTERFLIES go through the ultimate makeover – from caterpillar to butterfly – in about the time it takes you to grow back a bad haircut. It's more fun to watch than a reality show.

Stinging nettles are the peacock caterpillar's favourite food, which means if you want to keep your caterpillar happy and healthy, you'll need to get some nettle leaves. Fortunately, they grow just about everywhere, but make sure you wear gloves and jeans not shorts.

THE GOAL:
To see a peacock caterpillar transform into a butterfly.

THE EQUIPMENT:
- peacock butterfly egg or caterpillar
- pesticide-free stinging nettle plant
- a container with a perforated lid, preferably one with clear sides
- good-size twigs with a few branches
- paper towels

If you really want to hatch a butterfly but the closest you can get to a field or meadow is the potted plant on your windowsill, try a science hobby shop or online science shop. Most of them sell complete butterfly-raising kits.

THE SKILL:

1 Obtain a caterpillar. You can do this in one of three ways.

Find it in the wild. To do this, get to know the stinging nettle, the plant peacock caterpillars eat. If you check under its leaves in warm weather, you will probably find more caterpillars than you know what to do with.

Look for peacock eggs, which you can also find on the undersides of nettle leaves. Carefully remove the whole leaf with the egg on it. Wrap the leaf stem in a damp paper towel. Butterfly eggs typically hatch anywhere from three to twelve days after being laid.

You will need nettle leaves to feed the caterpillar. Don't forget to wear gloves to avoid being stung.

Purchase a butterfly-raising kit.

2 Once you're home, don't dilly-dally, prepare a habitat that will give your little insect the best chance of survival. The essential elements are a container, food, twigs and paper towels. (Hopefully that doesn't describe your bedroom.)

Use a large, clean, ventilated container of clear glass or plastic so you have an unobstructed front-row view of the process. An unused aquarium (empty of water, of course) or terrarium with a fine mesh screen on top is ideal. Failing this, take a cardboard box and staple clear

clingfilm around the edges,
then punch holes in it for
ventilation and turn it on its
side so you can see inside.

Place the twigs in the
container.

Lay damp paper towels
on the bottom to maintain the moist environment butterflies
like. The towels will also collect the droppings, making
your daily cleaning easier.

Don't put more than two or three eggs or caterpillars
in the container at once – even they need some space.

Keep a steady supply of nettle leaves on hand, as
the caterpillar will need to feed on them for about
four weeks. It is important that the nettles are always
fresh. Like you, butterflies-in-the-making aren't fond of
dried-out food.

You don't need to provide water since they get it from
their food.

3 Place the egg or caterpillar in your lovingly prepared habitat.

4 Clean out the droppings and replace the paper towels
once a day.

5 Keep the habitat somewhere convenient for making
frequent observations. Once the caterpillar has been
chomping down for three or four weeks, here's what
should happen:

The caterpillar will climb up one of the twigs and hang upside down from either the twig or the lid of the container.

The caterpillar will shed its skin and begin turning into a pupa, called a chrysalis or cocoon. This will take only a few hours at most. Once the cocoon is finished, you won't need to provide any more food.

The pupa hardens to protect the developing caterpillar. A peacock's pupa is quite bright green with darker dots. If yours turn out to be brown, you've got another butterfly that also likes nettles, such as a small tortoiseshell.

On the day the butterfly chooses to emerge, usually in the mid-morning, the cocoon will split open and the new peacock will emerge. No bloodcurdling roar, no tremendous tearing sound – butterflies are all about grace. Incidentally, all the butterflies that live on stinging nettles are beautiful.

6 You should release your butterfly into the wild within a day or two of its debut, as long as the temperature is above 13°C. Reach in and gently hold the butterfly's four wings together (it won't hurt either one of you!) then place it on a flower or plant. Wait and watch it fly off. Even though he probably won't write, know that he was grateful for your nurturing.

If you're not crazy about the idea of raising peacocks but are crazy about seeing them, try to attract them to your garden in some or all of the following ways:

- Plant stinging nettles if your parents permit it. These attract comma, red admiral and small tortoiseshell butterflies as well as peacocks.
- Plant flowers of certain shapes. Butterflies need a surface on which to land. Daisies, azaleas, zinnias, black-eyed Susans and sunflowers are beautiful bets.
- Plant flowers of certain colours. Butterflies are more fashion-conscious than you might realize. They tend to prefer purple, orange and yellow.
- Plant flowers with strong scents. The more fragrant, the better.
- Plant flowers that bloom at different times so the butterflies will have reason to visit throughout the season.
- Call out to them in butterfly language, if you know it. (Success rate for this method is pitifully low.)
- Dress like a butterfly and flap around your garden. Whether or not this attracts butterflies, it will surely keep most neighbours away.

If stinging nettles put you off, look for cabbage white caterpillars on nasturtium leaves. They're not such beautiful butterflies but they're just as interesting.

KIDSKILL #25
CATCH A SHOOTING STAR

WITH YOUR EYES, THAT IS. You can't catch a falling or shooting star (really a meteor) in your hands because it is a piece of intergalactic dust that gets burned up when it enters Earth's upper atmosphere. But you can watch it fall.

THE GOAL:
To get a front row seat for a meteor shower and make a wish.

You can see falling stars with your naked eyes, no telescope needed. However, the rest of you should not be naked.

THE EQUIPMENT:
- eyes
- reclining chair or blanket
- unobstructed view of the heavens
- a night during the second week of August

The darker your surroundings, the clearer any meteor shower will be. Moonlight and artificial light from streetlights, houses and so on can get in the way of seeing meteors. So can friends with large heads, so position yourself accordingly.

THE SKILL:

1 Every summer the Perseid meteor shower makes its annual appearance in the skies between the last week in July and the end of the second week in August. Viewing is usually best around August 12, so pick that night if you can, but also have a rain date.

2 Check the newspaper or search online for 'Perseids' and the current year to learn what nights and times will offer the best viewing. After 10 p.m. is usually when the show really starts, so you should probably include your parents in the planning. They'll like that.

3 Go outside at the suggested time. The shower often gives its best show after midnight – sometimes quite late (or early, depending on how you look at it).

You don't need to stay up the whole night waiting. Go to sleep when you're tired, but don't forget to set your alarm first. Have everything you want to bring outside ready by the door so you don't have to fumble around to find anything in the middle of the night. Also, since you'll be in a groggy state, try to remember why you're getting up and don't head off to school.

4 Spread out a blanket or set up a sunlounger in a peacefully dark spot. Get cosy.

Spotting an unexpected shooting star zip across the dark sky is exhilarating, but so is watching one you know is coming. Make it even more thrilling by building a party around it! Invite friends over to watch with you.

No worries if you don't know your south-wests from your north-easts. If it's not a cloudy or strongly moonlit night, you won't have to look long before you see your first meteor.

5 Scan the north-east region of the night sky. Don't concentrate on any one spot. You'll have better luck spying shooting stars if you relax your eyes.

6 Don't fret if you doze off for a moment. At their peak, the Perseids can send as many as sixty shooting stars per hour past your eyes. Another star will be along soon enough. And there's always next August. . . .

Take note that you are watching a meteor shower — not a meteoroid shower or a meteorite shower. They're all different things. A meteoroid is the chunk of space rock when it's still floating through space. A meteor is a bit of a meteoroid that enters Earth's atmosphere and burns up. A meteorite is a chunk large enough to survive the insanely hot drop through the sky and land on Earth.

CONCLUSION

Okay, you've finished the book.

You have no excuse.

You can't possibly have a boring summer now.

So stop complaining you have nothing to do. Just flip back to any page and get started.

If you manage to complete every activity before September, you are in an elite club. You will return to school with all the signs of a superstar summer: a sore tongue (from bird calling), palms with grass imprints (from hand-walking), a callused thumb (from stone skimming), wobbly legs (weak from chasing the ice-cream van), scraped knees (from tree climbing), a big bunch of new friends (from pizza-making), and most importantly, a red belly (from belly-flopping, of course).

Marc Tyler Nobleman is a writer and cartoonist whose work has appeared in more than 100 publications, including *The Wall Street Journal, Barron's, Forbes, Good Housekeeping,* and *The New York Daily News.* He is the author of more than 40 books and a dedicated fact compiler.

Dave Borgenicht is the co-author of the bestselling books in the Worst Case Scenario Survival Handbook series. He is also the publisher of Quirk Books, a book publisher dedicated to publishing "books with a sense of humour, but not necessarily humour books". He and his brother perfected the skills in this book over years of torture and torment — suffice to say, they are professional wedgiers. He lives in Philadelphia, US, with his wife and children.

Joe Borgenicht is a writer and producer. He is the co-author of a number of books, including The Baby Owner's Manual, The Action Hero's Handbook, The Action Heroine's Handbook, and The Reality TV Handbook. Joe has produced several television pilots. He lives in Salt Lake City, US, with his wife and son.

Matt Phillips has been doodling ever since he could hold a pen without poking himself; nothing too fancy or serious, just funny little doodles: bunnies, alligators, fish, and people without ears. With practise (mostly during maths class), Matt got to the point that he could draw just about anything that he wanted, even people with ears. The best thing is that Matt still draws funny little pictures all the time — and he actually does it for a living! Matt's doodles can be found in books, magazines, ads, food courts, and in little scrunched-up pieces of paper all around his drawing board. He lives in Georgia, US, with his wonderful wife, their big mutt, two little chihuahuas, and a cat that nobody ever sees.